KT-117-710

Will Technology Really Change Education?

From Blackboard to Web

Todd W. Kent • Robert F. McNergney

CORWIN PRESS, INC.
A Sage Publications Company
Thousand Oaks, California

For information:

Corwin Press, Inc.
A Sage Publications Company
2455 Teller Road
Thousand Oaks, California 91320
E-mail: order@corwinpress.com

SAGE Publications Ltd.
6 Bonhill Street
London EC2A 4PU
United Kingdom

SAGE Publications India Pvt. Ltd.
M-32 Market
Greater Kailash I
New Delhi 110 048 India

Printed in the United States of America

Library of Congress Cataloging-in-Publication Data

Kent, Todd W.
    Will technology really change education?: From blackboard to
Web / by Todd W. Kent and Robert F. McNergney.
        p.   cm.—(Critical issues in teacher education)
    Includes bibliographical references and index.
        ISBN 0-8039-6655-5 (cloth: acid-free paper)
        ISBN 0-8039-6656-3 (pbk.: acid-free paper)
        1. Educational technology—United States.   I. McNergney, Robert F.
    II. Title.   III. Series.
    LB1028.3 .K446   1998
    371.33—ddc21   98-40131

This book is printed on acid-free paper.

99   00   01   02   03   04   05   7   6   5   4   3   2   1

Editorial Assistant:	Julia Parnell
Production Editor:	Wendy Westgate
Editorial Assistant:	Nevair Kabakian
Cover Designer:	Tracy Miller
Typesetter:	Lynn Miyata

Contents

 Preface

Though some people may want to sidestep the issue, technology will continue to play an increasingly prominent role in education in the years to come. Our aim in this volume is to help teacher educators inform themselves on the problems, issues, and questions raised by current efforts to infuse computer technology into educational systems. As advocates tout the potential of technology and warn of disaster if educators drag their feet on its use, very little has been written about how technology might influence the interactions that occur among teachers and students. We address central questions concerning what we know about the use of technology, historical patterns of technology adoption by schools, how technology might be adapted to instructional models, and what the future might hold for teachers and teacher educators.

This book was commissioned by the American Association of Colleges for Teacher Education. Presumably, members of the publications committee wish to reinforce the long-standing commitment of the organization to encourage professional practice based on reason and knowledge. While we claim no corner on these commodities, we write to urge the use of existing knowledge to guide work with technologies and to encourage the profession to continue to enlarge what we know in this important area.

We thank Edward and Mary Ducharme, editors of the *Journal of Teacher Education* and professors at Drake University, for encouraging us to undertake this writing task. We also thank Allen Glenn, professor and dean at the University of Washington, for his helpful suggestions on an earlier draft of the manuscript. Our colleagues at The Hitachi Foundation have been most generous in their support of our evolving use of educational technology, and we are grateful for their assistance. Thanks too must go to Aileen Nonis, doctoral candidate at the University of Virginia, for a number of helpful references.

We use Chapter 1 to provide teacher educators with a set of questions to guide their thinking about technology and its use in classrooms. Many critics have argued that the successful use of technology in schools may depend on how well schools of education model technology use and prepare teachers to apply technology in their own classrooms. In Chapter 2, we examine current practice and thinking on technology. We provide information on how technology is being applied in schools and the rationales that are driving its use. We describe the role of technology in teacher education and the role of teacher education in influencing technology use in schools.

In Chapter 3, we discuss the successes and failures of previous attempts to integrate technologies into schools. We divide the discussion into two parts: the poor reception of "high technologies" (film, radio, and television) and the success of modest "low technologies" (textbooks, the chalkboard, and the overhead projector). The discussion focuses on salient characteristics relevant to current technologies.

In Chapter 4, we describe how technology can complement and supplement models of instruction. The discussion explores the potential of technology for enhancing the components common to any instructional model: (a) the purpose, (b) procedures of implementation, (c) the teacher's principles of reaction, (d) the social and technological systems necessary for implementation, and (e) provisions for evaluation.

We finish with Chapter 5, which foreshadows what the future might hold for teacher education. Some examples of current use provide the basis for what we believe is reasonable speculation.

The discussion is guided by the potential for teachers and teacher educators to shape this vision of the future.

We seek to view technology from the perspective of individuals who are interested in how teaching and learning might be enhanced by the machines and software that are becoming part of our daily lives. Instead of touting reform, we want to encourage attention to the relationship of technology to the interactions that occur between teacher and students and among students themselves.

About the Authors

Todd W. Kent is the Associate Director for the Teacher Preparation Program at Princeton University. He works closely with student teachers and is co-instructor of a course on teaching theory and methodology. He graduated from the University of Virginia in 1997 with a doctorate in educational evaluation; he also holds a master's degree in the social foundations of education from the University of Virginia and a bachelor's degree in economics from Princeton University. His specialty is the use of technology in teacher education and classroom instruction. He has taught courses on the use of computers and other media to preservice teachers and has been involved in several projects combining case-based instruction with telecommunication technology. He has authored a CD-ROM presentation of teaching cases as a companion to a textbook, and has written several book chapters on the use of technology in case-based teaching. Before entering higher education, he worked at an independent school in Maryland, where he enjoyed a variety of responsibilities, including teaching middle and high school science, heading the science department, and directing the upper school division.

Robert F. McNergney is Professor in the Curry School at the University of Virginia, where he teaches courses in foundations, evaluation, writing for publication, and research on teaching. He also teaches a set of Internet-based courses with colleagues in the United States, Canada, and Scandinavia. He has been a faculty member at the State University of New York, Potsdam, and at the University of Minnesota, Minneapolis. He has also taught and coached in public schools in Iowa and

Vermont. He is the coauthor of two books and editor of four, and his writing has appeared in the *Handbook of Research on Teacher Education, Educational Researcher, Journal of Teacher Education,* the *Washington Post,* and the *New York Times.* For 3 years, he coauthored the "Research Clues" column for *NEA Today.* He serves on the Technology Committee for the American Association of Colleges for Teacher Education, edits the *Division K Newsletter* in the American Educational Research Association, and chairs the Commission on Case-Method Teaching and Learning for the Association of Teacher Educators.

We are grateful to our families for their patience
and support through the writing of this narrative.
We also thank our students
for keeping us mindful of the future.

CHAPTER ONE

Using Technology in Education

An Introduction to Expectations and Reality

New educational technologies promise to change forever the way students learn and teachers teach—yet again. Support for the instructional use of computers continues to increase. A recent special report in *Education Week* states that spending on educational technology could top $5 billion in the 1997-98 school year. The same report cautions that a lack of research and a dearth of data promise unclear results from these expenditures (Trotter, 1997). President Clinton has noted that his 1997 State of the Union address contained more discussion of education than any previous such address. In the 1997 address, the president outlined a 10-point plan for improving education that included wiring every school in the United States to the Internet before the year 2000 (Applebome, 1997). Six months earlier, Clinton used the forum of his acceptance speech for the 1996 presidential nomination to proclaim, "I want to build a bridge to the 21st century in which we expand opportunity through education, where computers are as much a part of the classroom as blackboards."

Such high-profile attention to the promising role of technology in education repeats a historical pattern that began with the emergence of an American textbook industry in the mid-1800s and continued more recently with the introduction of educational television shortly after World War II. Wave after wave of technology reform in education has left many unfulfilled promises; the few

1

technologies that have had lasting impacts on the classroom include such high-tech wizardry as the printed textbook, the chalkboard, and the overhead projector. More complex technologies—film, radio, and television—never realized their imagined potential in education. Although these technologies can still be found in some classrooms, their use is minimal and sporadic. On the whole, glittering technology has had little influence in the classroom. In summarizing a study of technology in education during the past century, Cuban (1986) states:

> This study illustrates that the search for improving classroom productivity through technological innovations has yielded very modest changes in teacher practice without any clear demonstration that instruction is any more effective or productive after the introduction of radio, films, instructional television, or computers. (p. 109)

Teachers and, perhaps more important, teacher educators must sort through the exaggerated claims and public rhetoric to decide how much time, energy, and money should be directed toward the integration of technology with classroom instruction.

In this volume, we examine what the current push for classroom computers means for teacher educators. We focus on four questions of importance to teacher educators who want to understand the current context of educational technology. The first question we address is, What do we know about the current use of technology in education? In Chapter 2, we review the current state of technology use and the supporting research base to provide a measure of proportion that may be lost in all the industry claims and political posturing that direct precious resources toward purchasing new technologies for schools. Without question, the use of technology in classrooms is growing every day. How fast is this growth, and in what direction are school systems and teacher preparation programs moving? What does current research say about technology use? What are the instructional implications of our current knowledge base? As implied by the *Education Week* article cited earlier, many of these questions have vastly unsatisfying answers. Yet we do know something about technology and its use, and educational decisions should be informed by what we currently know.

Our second question is, How does the current push for computer technologies compare with the histories of previous technologies in educational reform? The historical context provided in Chapter 3 demonstrates that there are many similarities and some differences between current and past technologies. Although many have tried to do so, no one can predict with any certainty the long-term effects on education of current computer and telecommunication technologies. Understanding the historical patterns and the salient characteristics of successful technologies, however, will help us to gain important perspective on the current call to digitize education.

The third question we address is, How can we use knowledge of teaching to guide our use of technology? In Chapter 4, we describe a basic framework for examining technologically assisted models of instruction. The framework describes how technology might complement a model's purpose, its procedures of implementation, the teacher's principles of reaction, the social and technological systems necessary for implementation, and provisions for evaluation.

We finish with a fourth question that looks toward the future: What role might technology play in the future of teacher education? Perelman (1993) argues that future technologies will cause the demise of schools as we know them, and along with schools will go teacher education. Even if Perelman is only partially accurate, what are some of the implications of such radical change for the present practice of teacher education? What organizations and models might replace schools and teacher education programs as we know them? How might teacher educators prepare themselves and their young colleagues to participate in a technologically sophisticated future? We offer responses to these questions in Chapter 5, where we also speculate about the emergence and influence of new technologies on educational practice.

CHAPTER TWO

Technology and Teacher Education

Current Use and Knowledge

We have to believe in free will.
We've got no choice.

—Isaac Bashevis Singer

Some people may want to sidestep technology, but it will play an increasingly prominent role in classroom instruction in the coming decades. Perhaps more than any other factor, the current training of preservice teachers will be pivotal in determining the future role of technology in education (Byrum & Cashman, 1993). States are beginning to include new technologies in learning standards for all disciplines, thus increasing the pressure for teacher competence in this area. If technology is to be integrated successfully into classroom instruction, teacher educators must be able to exhibit successful technology use in preservice course work (Beichner, 1993).

The use of technology by schoolchildren necessarily depends on the ability of teachers to integrate technology into their teaching. Preservice education can provide rising teachers with the confidence and knowledge required to use the technological tools available to them. In considering how best to prepare teachers, we must first answer a basic question: What knowledge do we have about the current use of technology in education that might guide us in preparing teachers to use technology in tomorrow's classrooms? In this chapter we examine the emerging trends in technology use and the current thinking on the integration of technology and instruction. It is impossible, however, to discuss the use of technology in preservice education adequately without first considering how technology is currently used in schools.

Technology Use in Schools

A lack of substantive research plagues any discussion of the current use of technology in education. In an effort to help fill this gap, *Education Week* published "Technology Counts" (1997b), a report on the use of technology in schools in all 50 states.

> Scholars have yet to examine fully the growing use of technology to let students take control of their own learning. For more established applications, research shows that some provide unquestionable results, while others remain unproved. *Education Week* quotes a draft federal study by the Washington, DC-based American Institutes for Research that concludes, "At this point, there are more claims about what technology can do than there are well-designed evaluations with conclusive findings." ("Technology Counts," 1997a, p. 2)[1]

Despite the inconclusive research base, support for future investments in technology persists, or, more accurately, rages. A presidential report on the use of technology in K-12 education provides a rationale for investing in technology based on the constructivist zeitgeist apparent in many educational reform initiatives. The report describes technology as supporting the current pedagogical shift in education toward the constructivist paradigm. The major elements of that paradigm are described by the report as follows:

- Greater attention is given to the acquisition of higher-order thinking and problem-solving skills, with less emphasis on the assimilation of a large body of isolated facts.
- Basic skills are learned not in isolation, but in the course of undertaking (often on a collaborative basis) higher-

level "real-world" tasks whose execution requires the integration of a number of such skills.

- Information resources are made available to be accessed by the student at that point in time when they actually become useful in executing the particular task at hand.
- Fewer topics may be covered than is the case within the typical traditional curriculum, but these topics are often explored in greater depth.
- The student assumes a central role as the active architect of his or her own knowledge and skills, rather than passively absorbing information proffered by the teacher. (President's Committee of Advisors on Science and Technology, 1997, p. 16)

Technology, the report's authors argue, can support such approaches to teaching in a number of ways. They list some possible uses of computers and computer networks by teachers to support constructivist learning:

- Monitor, guide, and assess the progress of their students.
- Maintain portfolios of student work.
- Prepare (both computer-based and conventional) materials for use in the classroom.
- Communicate with students, parents, and administrators.
- Exchange ideas, experiences, and curricular materials with other teachers.
- Consult with experts in a variety of fields.
- Access remote databases and acquire educational software over the Internet.
- Further expand their own knowledge and professional capabilities. (p. 17)

There is abundant anecdotal evidence of the successful use of technology in the classroom—the presidential report offers nine examples, most of which involve minority or low-income populations. These selective views support the contention that technology can help schools achieve such desirable outcomes as improved test scores, reduced failure rates, lower absenteeism, fewer student withdrawals, increased graduation rates, improved job placement rates, and overall improvement in motivation.

The *Education Week* report also describes a lack of sufficient descriptive data to portray the current level of technology use in education. Researchers may struggle in measuring current usage, but the public is unequivocal in its desire to see more technology in our schools. A public opinion survey done for *Education Week* by the Milken Family Foundation (1997) found the following:

> Americans overwhelmingly understand that technology can play a vital role in education, especially in providing access to information and preparing students for the jobs of the future. 85 percent of voters surveyed believe that schools well-equipped with technology have a major advantage over schools that are poorly equipped. 74 percent say that technology will have a positive effect on education, because it will provide students with equal access to information and knowledge. All demographic groups are optimistic that technology will break down society's barriers, not increase them. (p. 1)

Such public and political support for technology use generates financial support. *Education Week* predicted that spending on technology for the 1997-98 school year would be approximately $5.2 billion, an increase of nearly $1 billion over the previous year. Although technology spending continues to gain momentum, current expenditures represent only 2% of total education spending. Additionally, the federal government, through the Telecommunications Act of 1996, supports education technology spending with a program of "E-rate" discounts for schools purchasing telecommunications services. The *Education Week* report estimates that this program will add $10 billion to educational technology spending from 1997 to 2001. Increased spending, supported by favorable public opinion, suggests that pressure on teachers to use technology will continue to mount in the foreseeable future.

Not surprisingly, some critics decry the spending on technology. Samuel G. Sava, the executive director of the National Association of Elementary School Principals, has stated:

> I'm very concerned over the rush to purchase hardware when we do not have enough evidence on how best to use computers to help youngsters achieve in reading, mathematics, writing, et cetera. My second concern is that a number of school systems, in order to purchase the hardware, have begun to eliminate such key programs as the arts. (quoted in Trotter, 1997, p. 7)

Another concern of educators is the quality of information that can be found on the Internet. In a recent poll by MCI Corporation, more than 60% of teachers surveyed expressed concern about the content available on the Internet. Most teachers wanted instructional materials based on research and presented by respected educational groups (Trotter & Zehr, 1998). Such sentiments, however, seem to have little effect on the momentum of the current support for technology use. Because support for increasing technology use in schools increases in the absence of effectiveness data, the relevant issue may not be whether technology is effective, but when and how it can be used most advantageously. This perspective is supported by Stephen Marcus, codirector of the South Coast Writing Project and a researcher at the University of California, Santa Barbara:

> Where technology is used wisely and where the teachers are given the right kinds of support and training and the right kind of equipment, then [they] are able to actually implement some of the best theory and practice regarding the teaching of writing. Students are more willing to do more editing, to spend more time reviewing their text and improving it. But to provide a computer and think that students' writing will somehow magically improve—that's just wishful thinking. (quoted in Viadero, 1997b, p. 13)

The *Education Week* report describes several features shared by schools that managed to sustain their investments and the use of technology over time:

- A principal and district administrators committed to the project

- A belief on the part of educators that technology is a way to extend the curriculum and to support education reforms—and some knowledge of how to do it
- The involvement of teachers in schoolwide instructional decisions
- Adequate allocation of time and money for staff development—on site—and for follow-up support
- A history of openness to educational innovations
- A link between technology and district or state curricular standards—and rewritten frameworks to reflect technology's role (Cradler, as described in Viadero, 1997a, p. 16)

Additionally, four factors appear to encourage the use of computers by teachers and students:

- Collegiality among computer users
- Resources available for staff development and computer coordination
- Smaller class sizes
- School support for using computers for meaningful activities, such as producing the school yearbook and newspaper (Becker, as described in Zehr, 1997, p. 28; see also Viadero, 1997a, p. 16)

Identifying such variables may help educators to plan the integration of technology into existing programs. As with any educational program, the influences on program outcomes are numerous and can differ substantially from one environment to another.

The *Education Week* report also collected statistics describing the prevalence of technology in schools. The statistics in the report reveal wide variation among states. On average, 70% of schools nationwide have access to the Internet. The proportion varies from a low of 44% for Mississippi to a high of 92% for Vermont. On average, there are 21 students per multimedia computer in the United States. Kansas leads the technology pack with only 11 students per machine; Louisiana lags behind with 36 students per computer. The location of computers in schools is evenly split between the classroom and the computer lab. On average, 45% of the computers in schools are found in individual classrooms; 46% are located in labs. The location of computers is influenced by grade level. For example, 29% of fourth graders have access to two or more computers in their classrooms, but only 12% of eighth graders do. More eighth graders have access to computers situated in labs (44%) than do their fourth grade counterparts (29%).

Currently, 32 states have technology requirements for teacher licensure. Only 15% of teachers across the United States have received 9 or more hours of technology training. As might be expected from this low level of training, the average level of computer use remains low. Nationwide, 57% of eighth graders report never or hardly ever using computers for mathematics. Only 15% use computers once or twice a week; 12% report using computers nearly every day.

Without question, teacher education influences the level of use of technology in the classroom. The *Education Week* report notes that teachers need more training in technology:

> Only half the teachers surveyed by an educational software company this year said they had the right training to integrate technology regularly into lessons. Only one in five report using a computer for teaching, according to a federal survey. With billions being spent on equipment, some experts contend the adeptness of teachers in using it may hold back technology's promise. ("Technology Counts," 1997a, p. 2)

As in the use of other high technologies in the classroom, teachers possess the key to the success of the use of current computer technologies. Computers, software, and related technologies must be adaptable to the instructional needs of teachers and to the daily realities of classroom life, but teachers must also have adequate training and support to use these technologies.

Technology and Teacher Education

To understand teachers' needs with regard to technology in the classroom, one must understand the role of teacher education.

A recent report to President Clinton on the use of technology in K-12 education states:

> In order to make effective use of educational technology, teachers will have to master a variety of powerful tools, redesign their lesson plans around technology-enhanced resources, solve the logistical problem of how to teach a class full of students with a smaller number of computers, and take on a complex new role in the technologically transformed classroom. Yet teachers currently receive little technical, pedagogic or administrative support for these fundamental changes, and few colleges of education adequately prepare their graduates to use information technologies in their teaching. As a result, most teachers are left largely on their own as they struggle to integrate technology into their curricula. (President's Committee of Advisors on Science and Technology, 1997, p. 47)

The report goes on to describe the essential role that teacher education can play in helping teachers meet the demands of an evolving technological school culture:

> Over 200,000 new teachers enter the profession each year, and there is a 50 percent turnover in the teaching force approximately every 15 years. While advances in underlying technologies, educational software, and pedagogic methods will result in an ongoing need for in-service training, colleges of education have a valuable opportunity to introduce future teachers to the use of educational technology before the demands of an actual teaching position begin to impinge on the time available for such training. (p. 53)

Although many perceive an opportunity for teacher education to take leadership in giving teachers the knowledge and skills they need to use technology effectively, few programs have seized the initiative. Byrum and Cashman (1993) examined the integration of technology in six midwestern schools of education and found that 78% of the preservice teachers had taken at least one course in which computers had been used instructionally, and 83% of the students felt comfortable with their abilities to integrate computers into their classroom instruction. On a less favorable note, they also found that only 58% of the preservice teachers had been in education classes in which computers had been discussed. The majority of those students reported that the discussion had taken place in a technology class. Many respondents (91%) also stated that their preference for computer integration lay in lower-order learning, such as drill and practice. Most of the students' exposure to computers came in a single technology class. There was a notable lack of modeling for technology use in the teacher education programs. Preservice teachers also believed that their own lack of training would pose problems for them in their professional lives.

Byrum and Cashman's (1993) study demonstrates the pitfalls of isolating technology instruction to single courses. Integration of technology into instruction is a complex process that cannot be captured in any single "how-to" course. For preservice teachers to learn how to integrate technology into their own teaching, it is reasonable to think that technology should first be integrated successfully into professional education course work.

Longitudinal qualitative data taken from classrooms in the Apple Classrooms of Tomorrow (ACOT) project indicate the complexity of technology acquisition for teachers. Dwyer, Ringstaff, and Sandholtz (1990) found that these data reveal five phases of teacher behavior during the process of technology integration. The impact of technology on classroom instruction increases as teachers move through these phases. The first phase, *entry,* reflects teachers' concerns and issues involved with technical and managerial issues as they become familiar with new technology. The style of classroom instruction during the entry phase is predominantly the same as before the introduction of technology. The *adoption* phase follows the entry phase. Here teachers focus less on technical issues and more on how to integrate technology with instruction. The adoption phase shows an increase in the use of technology in the classroom, but teachers use the technology to support the same instructional patterns that existed before the introduction of technology. (In the case of the ACOT classroom, these patterns consisted of lectures, recitation, and individual seatwork.) In the third phase, *adaptation,* there is an emphasis on the use of technology as a productivity tool. As students become more proficient at typing, computers become a means for attaining speed and efficiency in instructional activities.

Appropriation, the fourth phase identified in the ACOT study, generally becomes apparent in the second year of technology introduction. In this phase, teachers show personal mastery of the technology as they begin to introduce new instructional strategies in their classrooms. Team teaching, project-based instruction, and individually paced instruction emerged as characteristics in the ACOT classrooms. The final phase, *invention,* involves the creation of new learning environments that differ radically from previous forms of instruction. Teachers come to view learning as an active, creative, and socially interactive process. Control of the learning process shifts from teacher-centered practice to a more student-directed process. During the invention phase, teachers begin to question their previously held conceptions regarding learning. The ACOT study also found that certain kinds of support help speed the evolution of teachers through these phases. Effective support includes mentors who are more experienced in using technology with instruction, opportunities to reflect, and encouragement of teachers to question beliefs about teaching and learning (Apple Computer, 1995).

Research on technology and teacher instruction suggests that teacher education programs need to model technology use if preservice teachers are to acquire the necessary expertise to integrate technology into their own teaching. The ACOT program argues that teachers must move through certain phases before successful technology integration can take place. Such opportunities do not exist in the context of a single course.

A recent report by the National Council for Accreditation of Teacher Education (1997) describes the current state of technology use in teacher education programs:

> Bluntly, a majority of teacher preparation programs are falling far short of what needs to be done. Not using technology much in their own research and teaching, teacher education faculty have insufficient understanding of the demands on classroom teachers to incorporate technology into their teaching. Many do not fully appreciate the impact technology is having on the way work is accomplished. They undervalue the significance of technology and treat it as merely another topic about which teachers should be informed. (p. 6)

The same report describes some possible reasons for a sluggish response to new technologies in teacher preparation programs:

> The reasons for these deficiencies in teacher education programs are relatively easy to explain, if difficult to excuse. First of all, many teacher education programs lack the hardware and software essential to strong programs. Teacher education programs often are given low priority for special technology funding on their campuses and therefore are denied essential technology. Second, many teacher education faculty lack the knowledge and skill to incorporate technology into their own teaching. Similar to P-12 teachers, they have not been provided the training they need to use technology successfully. Third, a majority of teacher education departments and colleges have not been able to invest in the technical support required to maintain a high quality technology program. Fourth, some higher education faculty are out of touch with what is happening in schools. They have little understanding of the vast changes that are occurring in P-12 classrooms as a result of the introduction of technology and how they must change their own instruction to stay abreast of changes in the schools. Finally, teacher education programs are driven by an academic culture that rewards and recognizes individuality among faculty. There are few incentives for bringing faculty together around a common vision about what the teacher education program should be. (p. 7)

A recent survey sponsored by the American Association of Colleges for Teacher Education supports the perspective that teacher education programs could be doing much more with technology. Only 28% of the programs surveyed require students to design and deliver instruction that incorporates various technologies during student teaching, and only 41% of the programs require student teachers to demonstrate use of at least one technology during student teaching; 31% of the programs have no technology requirements at all (Persichitte, Tharp, & Caffarella, 1997).

Until teacher education programs integrate technology, preservice teachers will have no opportunity to begin moving through the phases described by Dwyer et al. (1990). Additionally, the work of Byrum and Cashman (1993) demonstrates the importance of modeling and the pitfall of isolating technology instruction in specific courses. If state certification agencies and local hiring authorities expect teachers to demonstrate intelligent use of technology, teacher education programs need to provide them with opportunities to observe and practice.

A 1995 report by the Office of Technology Assessment (OTA) emphasizes the importance of modeling as well as the importance of opportunities to see and use technology in educational settings:

> One conclusion to be drawn is that telling students about what is possible is not enough; they must see technology used by their instructors, observe uses of technological tools in classrooms, and practice teaching with technologies themselves if they are to use these tools effectively in their own teaching. (p. 185)

The same report comments on the quality of technology instruction. In a survey of recent graduates, 40% reported that the education faculty used technology in courses. The report comments:

> However, an analysis of this is revealing: the areas that were most often reported as "taught about" were drill-and-practice applications and word processing. While half of recent graduates surveyed reported being prepared to teach with drill and practice, tutorials, games, and writing and publishing centers, less than one in 10 felt they could use such formats as multimedia packages, electronic presentations, collaborations over networks, or problem-solving software. Rarely were teacher education students asked to develop material or create lessons with technology. (p. 186)

The OTA report argues that technology can enhance the preservice experience by capturing the reality of the classroom through video and other media, by facilitating access to information and communication with experts in the field, and by supporting and enhancing traditional approaches to teacher-developed curriculum materials and instructional practices. Preservice education can prepare new teachers to use a range of technological tools and to do so in the most cost-effective way. Yet evidence on the use of technology in teacher education programs tends to be disappointing.

The OTA surveyed teacher preparation faculty to determine what barriers they face in using technology. Respondents noted time constraints, limited resources, their own comfort level and attitudes, and little institutional encouragement for technology use. In regard to faculty attitudes, the report notes, "it is not surprising that faculty members agree technology is important while simultaneously presuming it is a 'topic' that will be covered somewhere in the curricula other than in the courses they teach." It goes on, "Since the majority of teacher education faculty completed graduate programs and taught in schools where technology was not a major part of the educational environment, it is not surprising that they tend to have limited experience with technologies for instruction" (p. 190). The report concludes that many faculty members' institutions provide little incentive for teacher educators to learn technology skills, and the pressure for institutionally valued research and writing leaves little time to invest in technology. Moreover, the report suggests that teacher education programs are more likely to be "have-nots" than "haves" in terms of technological resources devoted to faculty.

The OTA report describes three primary areas of teacher education instruction in regard to technology use: discussion about technology or demonstration of technology by the instructor, hands-on technology practice by the student, and professional practice in which students are exposed to classroom instruction using technology and have the opportunity to practice teaching with technology themselves. Of these three areas, professional practice is the most critical level of engagement. A study by Thomas, Larson, Clift, and Levin (1996) supports this premise:

> In our work with the *Teaching Teleapprenticeships* project, we have found that when technology topics are infused throughout meaningful, contextualized experiences in university and school settings, student teachers are more apt to embrace, model, use, and incorporate technology into their instructional planning and classroom organization. (p. 4)

These authors identify two essential components of their program: access and training. They define *access* as access to equipment and ongoing support and as access in terms of the ease with which e-mail, discussion groups, and other technology allow individuals to communicate with each other. Thomas et al. found that when the notion of training includes modeling by instructors, incorporating technology in content-related assignments, and providing an "on-call" support staff, the use of technology among faculty and students increases.

Cooper and Bull (1997) provide a framework to promote the use of technology in teacher preparation programs. They identify three general principles that contribute to a positive environment for nurturing technology use. First, schools should allow the use of technology to diffuse through a program rather than rely on coercive policies to win over reluctant faculty. Incentives such as instructional grants, release time, and graduate student support can encourage faculty members to adopt technology in their courses. Moreover, the influence of national and state standards, which are increasingly including technology components, will help move programs to integrate technology throughout the curriculum. Second, the integration of technology throughout the teacher preparation process is essential. The more prevalent and visible technology is, the better. Third, teacher preparation programs must aggressively pursue funding models that provide stability in financial support of technology. Cooper and Bull argue that a lack of systematic planning for technology funding causes teacher education programs to lag behind the technology initiatives currently embraced in K-12 programs.

Cooper and Bull (1997) also provide eight specific guidelines to help programs integrate technology into their programs:

1. Develop a vision of how technology fits the conceptual model of the program.

2. Support local schools' efforts to use technology and learn together.

3. Create a school of education culture that fosters exploration and a fearlessness about using and experimenting with technology.

4. Provide incentives for people to use technology.

5. If the program wants to encourage the use of particular software, provide that software for free while also allowing individuals to use software they want.

6. Support those who are using technology effectively and encourage them to share what they learn with other faculty members.

7. Invite all to participate and to shape the technology agenda.

8. Allow a sufficient gestation period before expecting results.

A developing consensus among education technologists values the integration of technology throughout the teacher education curriculum, as opposed to relying on specific courses to teach technology methods and skills.

A recent study supported by the American Association of Colleges for Teacher Education found technology to be present in nearly all teacher education programs (Persichitte, 1998). The overwhelming majority of teacher education programs had adequate infrastructure for supporting the use of information technologies. More than 95% of the respondents reported having faculty and students who were using technologies. A follow-up study identified examples of best practices and determined common characteristics across those programs. Three teacher preparation programs were selected: the University of Arkansas at Fayetteville, Graceland College in Iowa, and the University of Virginia's Curry School of Education. This study found that institutions with exemplary technology use in teacher education programs shared the following characteristics:

- Program experiences that infuse professor and student use of educational technologies throughout campus and field-based experiences
- Emphasis on the integration of a variety of educational technologies within the preservice experience
- Professor modeling and student practice with technology across the curricula
- Commitment to and support of the continued professional development of faculty use and integration of technologies
- Faculty emphasis on the current research associated with using technology for instructional purposes

- Use of technology to connect professors, preservice students, and K-12 students
- Efforts to support the achievement of state and/or content standards by supporting pedagogy with technology
- Use of the World Wide Web to develop multiple levels and types of student-teacher interactions
- Multimedia projects developed as part of the curriculum, but also required for integration within the field experience
- A consistent message that the primary importance of technology integration is instructional, but that personal skills must be developed before professional practice can change

Although these examples of best practices may have qualities in common, to succeed any model for using technology effectively must be adapted to the context and the people working within a given environment. Lessons from the implementation of past technologies may help provide insight for decisions on the use of contemporary technologies.

Note

1. This quote and all further quotes from this special issue of *Education Week* are reprinted with permission from *Education Week,* Vol. 17, No. 11, November 10, 1997.

CHAPTER THREE

Patterns of Change
The Historical Context
of Educational Technologies

*Teach the children everything from mathematics
to morality. . . . Sort o' swing the education in on
them so attractively that they'll want to go to
school. You'll have to lick 'em to keep 'em away.*
—Thomas Alva Edison

Thomas Edison was one of the most colorful and vocal proponents of educational technology. The above quotation represents the type of rhetoric Edison used to promote educational
films. His promotion of instructional films included the prediction
that film would completely revolutionize education and that someday the technology would replace textbooks. He promoted grandiose visions of how film would transform learning in schools, yet
those visions never materialized. Likewise, more contemporary individuals have predicted that computer technologies will transform the classroom environment as we know it. In his 1997 State
of the Union address, President Clinton presented a 10-point plan
to improve education, and his closing point focused on access to
telecommunication technology in our schools:

> Tenth: we must bring the power of the Information Age into
> all our schools. Last year, I challenged America to connect
> every classroom and library to the Internet by the year 2000,

so that, for the first time in history, a child in the most isolated rural town, the most comfortable suburb, the poorest
inner city school, will have the same access to the same
universe of knowledge.

Later in that same address, Clinton gave a small glimpse of the
power he associates with these new technologies:

> We must build the second generation of the Internet so our
> leading universities and national laboratories can commu-
> nicate at speeds 1000 times faster than today, to develop
> new medical treatments, new sources of energy, and new
> ways of working together. But we cannot stop there. As the
> Internet becomes our new town square, a computer in
> every home—a teacher of all subjects, a connection to all
> cultures—this will no longer be a dream, but a necessity.
> And over the next decade, that must be our goal.

Others present even more radical portrayals of the future
course of technology use in our culture and in our schools. Lewis
Perelman (1993) describes his own vision of impending technological change by comparing envisioned transformations in our
classrooms to changes we have already seen in other areas:

> So some people may still speak in the twenty-first century
> about "schools" and "colleges" and "students" and "teach-
> ers." But the hyper-learning systems of the imminent future
> in reality will bear less resemblance to old-fashioned class-
> rooms than the M1A1 Abrams tank bears to a Roman char-
> iot. (p. 51)

Perelman foresees a world of highly individualized learning,
where students will learn—and pay for their education—through
computer-supplied educational materials that are tailored to the
students' needs and interests. Gone will be the classrooms of today, where students learn roughly the same material in roughly the
same sequence. Students will construct their own learning
through electronic resources, and the role of the traditional
teacher will be obsolete.

By examining why such "high" technologies as film, radio, and television have largely failed to generate a substantial reform of education, we can better assess what weight to assign the visions of technology pundits like Perelman. Perhaps most important, such retrospection may help us answer the question of how the current push for integrating technology into schools might compare with the histories of previous technologies in educational reform. To address this question, we will follow three lines of thought. First, in a discussion of high technologies (film, radio, and television), we will identify the patterns of use and reasons for unmet expectations associated with each. Second, in a discussion of "low" technologies (textbooks, blackboard, overhead projector), we will examine why such simple tools have influenced classroom instruction to a far greater extent than the high technologies. And third, we will use these discussions as the context for a consideration of the characteristics of computer technologies most relevant to the lives of educators.

High Technologies: Film, Radio, and Television

Cuban (1986) identifies a common pattern that the introduction and use of past instructional technologies have tended to follow. He calls this pattern the "exhilaration/scientific-credibility/disappointment/teacher-bashing cycle" and describes convincingly how the histories of the high technologies of film, radio, and television consistently fit this pattern. The cycle begins with a period of excitement in which reformers—most often foundation executives, educational administrators, and wholesalers—tout new technologies as solutions for whatever ails the nation's schools. Shortly after the new technologies gain some attention, academics produce studies describing the effectiveness of the new tools. As the technologies fail to gain widespread acceptance in schools, new surveys document the disappointingly infrequent use of the technologies by educators. During the final phase of the cycle, teachers are criticized for resisting change and subverting the improvements made possible by the new technologies. Cuban argues that this cycle has been produced by a tension created through teaching reforms initiated by nonteachers who have consistently demonstrated a lack of understanding of the teacher's classroom perspective.

Are we currently in the midst of another exhilaration phase as described by Cuban? By examining lessons from past technologies, we might gain insight regarding our present struggle to find an effective role for technology in the classroom. A recent editorial in *Phi Delta Kappan* reminds us of the importance of remembering the past. In response to criticism of California's recent commitment of funds to equip public schools with computers, the author notes:

> It reminded me of the hopes many of us had for instructional television (ITV) in the mid-Seventies. But good ITV programming was not accompanied by effective training of teachers to use the new technology. So teachers simply turned on their classroom television sets for 15 minutes to entertain their students while they themselves graded papers. And that was that. . . . Americans have extremely short memories. And those who forget the past will continue to reinvent wheels that continue to fall off wagons. Ignorance of our own history gets us nowhere. (Gough, 1998, p. 642)

The federal government now provides funding, through its "E-dollar" program, to alleviate the costs for schools of getting wired to the Internet. These new Internet connections may provide exciting and meaningful learning opportunities for students, or the computers may simply be used by teachers for "edutainment," as in the case of ITV. The future role of computer technologies will be determined primarily by two factors: (a) whether teachers find value in the instructional possibilities offered by the new technologies, and (b) whether the pattern of implementation of the new technologies avoids the mistakes made with past technologies.

The high educational technologies share a number of attributes beyond the cycle identified by Cuban. In the following discussion we will identify those historical characteristics of past technologies most relevant for understanding the current role of computer technology in educational reform. We will then compare the characteristics of these largely unsuccessful high technologies and those of the more readily accepted low technologies.

Film

Film was introduced with great claims for its potential to influence the entire ethos of the classroom. After motion pictures were introduced in France in 1895, the following decades witnessed great efforts by governments, established businesses, and a growing entertainment industry to promote the acceptance of the use of film in education (Dockterman, 1988). Thomas Edison became an extremely vocal proponent of educational film, and he was not shy about making far-reaching claims for its effectiveness. Within a short time, an entire industry, including several new journals, formed to promote educational film. The instructional use of film became a symbol of progressive teaching approaches, and "the black window shades, silver screen, and 16mm projector lent an aura of modernity and innovativeness to classrooms" (Cuban, 1986, p. 12). Educational research during the 1920s and 1930s, although at times questionable in its methodology, largely convinced policy makers of the effectiveness of film as an instructional tool.

Use of film by classroom teachers never gained substantial momentum. Even when equipment and films were readily available, their presence in classrooms continued to be infrequent. In some instances, a few zealot individuals accounted for a disproportionate level of use:

> A study of 175 elementary teachers in New Haven, Connecticut, discovered that teachers ordered about fifteen hundred films in one year, but two-thirds of the orders came from twenty-five mediaphiles. When researchers investigated obstacles to the use of moving pictures, they pinpointed the teachers' lack of skills, the cost of purchase and upkeep of the equipment, and the inability to find the right fit between films and class lessons. (Tyack & Cuban, 1995, p. 123)

Critics lamented that teachers were unwilling to change their instructional practices adequately to take advantage of the promises offered by film. Cuban (1986) argues, however, that teachers have always been willing to change practice, and have done so with other low technologies, so long as they have perceived that the new technologies would help them address the problems they have identified. The problem is that reformers did not match the innovations to teachers' views of daily classroom realities.

The failure of particular technologies to take hold may well lie in their inability to address the perceptions and needs of teachers. The issue of quality also hindered the universal acceptance of film as a classroom fixture. Most film production investment was directed toward the entertainment industry, and relatively few films were made expressively for educational purposes. Although film was used sparingly in classrooms, and educational films were of questionable quality, the U.S. Army made effective use of film, especially during World War II, for instructional purposes. Describing an interview with Frances Keppel, who worked with army films during that time, Dockterman (1988) relates the importance of quality in the success of films for training:

> As Keppel tells it, they hired educational film producers to create these training movies. The results were horrible. They tried again, but this time they turned to commercial producers, to Hollywood, where they recruited the likes of Frank Capra. The costs of personnel and production soared, but it was war and the budget was unlimited. The second time around achieved excellent results. These films did the job. Keppel's point: quality software can be made available to schools, but only for a price. (p. 114)

In addition to problems with quality, the medium of film carries some unique physical constraints. To view a film, the instructor needs access to both the film and equipment to project the film. To preview a film for instructional use, the instructor needs access to the film, availability of equipment, a place to view the film, and enough free time to run the film in its entirety. It may be extremely difficult for teachers to preview and prepare lessons for a 90-minute film in a school day broken up into 50-minute periods. Finally, replaying particular segments of a film could be exceedingly cumbersome, and some teachers saw darkened rooms for viewing films as potentially problematic for classroom discipline (Dockterman, 1988).

No single factor can be blamed for film's lukewarm acceptance by classroom teachers. The medium's potential for engaging presentation and the ability to bring a wide range of content to the classroom were evidently outweighed by the negative qualities associated with film. The need for equipment and for darkened classrooms, the inability to vary the format of the film, difficulty with repeating and finding particular film segments, limited accessibility to films for viewing and previewing, the poor quality of film content, the lack of teacher training, and lack of understanding of classroom life by film advocates all contributed to film's poor reception.

Radio and Television

We combine discussion of radio and television because of the similarities these two media share as broadcast technologies. Radio promised to open classrooms to the world. It would allow students access to the finest teachers, the best authorities in every field, and the world's leaders. Radio was to become the "textbook of the air" (Darrow, 1932). Like film, however, radio never lived up to the potential envisioned by reformers.

The age of television gained great momentum in the years following World War II. Television had film's ability to combine visual images and sound, and televised content could be delivered with the immediacy enjoyed by radio. In a sense, television combined all the best aspects of the media that preceded it. The outcomes for educational television, however, were essentially the same as those for film and radio.

In 1952, the Federal Communications Commission reserved 242 television channels for educational use. In 1951, the Ford Foundation created the Fund for Adult Education and the Fund for the Advancement of Education, two entities that helped direct money and resources to educational broadcasting (Saettler, 1990). Never before had educational technology received such financial support. Some support for educational television was based in concern about predicted teacher shortages that emerged in the early 1950s. Media attention helped to create the perception that technology might soon start replacing teachers.

Despite several notable initiatives—in Hagerstown, Maryland; American Samoa; and elsewhere—educational television suffered the same unenthusiastic reception by classroom teachers as had film and radio. Two primary factors may have contributed to the demise of educational television: the lack of quality in programming and the "teacherless approach" to the medium.

Wagschal (1986) argues that proponents of computer technologies can profit from three lessons learned in the unsuccessful attempt to introduce television into classrooms. First, schools must set aside money for support beyond the expenditure on hardware. In the case of television, many schools failed to reserve financial resources for upkeep and maintenance. This problem is exacerbated with computer technologies because of the continual need for software and because the machines quickly become obsolete. The second lesson relates to training:

> At the same time, the problems of training teachers to use those computers as part of their daily routine have been even more confusing than those connected with television. Insofar as teachers have been trained at all, it has tended to be in the technical aspects of using computers—largely because no one has a good conception of what teachers should be doing with these machines in their classrooms. (p. 33)

The third lesson stems from teachers' attitudes toward the quality of software. Teachers were largely unhappy with the content and format of ITV programming. Although educational software has seen some improvement in recent years, teachers continue to voice doubts regarding the quality of educational applications and the content they find on the Internet. Wagschal believes these problems can be avoided if one guiding principle is followed: "Decisions regarding the appropriate place of computer technology in educating children must be made by individual teachers, because they are the only ones in a position to determine how that technology can fit into the daily routine of classroom life" (p. 34). Wagschal also believes that for teachers to gain technical competence, computers must be placed in the hands of the teachers.

The media of film, radio, and television all reinforced the idea of "teacher-proof" curricula by requiring the teacher to stop teaching while the medium was running. Moreover, students generally were unable to raise questions or have portions of the instruction repeated during the media portion of the lesson. The teacher had no control over the content or its presentation. These factors created a degree of inflexibility commonly associated with the high technologies.

Film, radio, and television shared some other problems as well, as viewed from the teachers' perspective. Nonteachers were the most vocal promoters of all three technologies. Teachers were seldom consulted or involved (especially in the early stages) in the adaptation of the medium to classroom use. The content and instructional implementation of these media reflected little understanding of the daily realities of the classroom teacher. All three technologies required substantial equipment, which inevitably led to problems with access, maintenance, and operation of the hardware. In each case, far more resources were devoted to development of the more lucrative commercial and entertainment markets for the medium, which was reflected in the poor quality of products offered for education. Radio and television, more so than film, had the additional disadvantage of scheduling conflicts with schools. Finally, all three technologies were passive—students simply watched and/or listened. With each technology, someone other than the classroom teacher created the instructional objectives and lesson delivery. These media lacked any interactivity and depended on the skill of the teacher to integrate the content with existing curriculum. In each case, the success of the medium was determined by how the teacher valued and used it in the classroom: "Inadequate or obsolete equipment, limited availability of a viable signal, awkward scheduling of broadcasts, and amateurish programs have persistently blocked teachers from increasing their usage of radio, film, and television" (Cuban, 1986, p. 53). Ironically, the most successful classroom technologies have been those that, because of their simplicity and flexibility, have escaped some of the problems associated with more complicated media.

 Low Technologies

"Low" technologies, tools that are relatively simple in their design and application, have had much greater influence on daily educational life than more complex high technologies. Cuban (1986) describes the characteristics of these successful technologies as follows: "The tools that teachers have added to their repertoire over time (e.g., chalkboard and textbooks) have been simple, durable, flexible, and responsive to teacher-defined problems in meeting the demand of daily instruction" (p. 58). The acceptance of a technology appears to depend on the degree to which it demonstrates pedagogical flexibility, supports teacher control, and is accessible. Low technologies address problems perceived by teachers and are adaptable to changing classroom environments and demands; thus they have gained acceptance and widespread use. In addition, these tools continue to place teachers at the center of the instructional process. Dockterman (1988) argues that, "whether termed flexible or general, the teacher dependent tools have a greater chance of gaining widespread acceptance while the teacherless (or teacher-proof) instruments will likely be turned down by all but a distinct minority" (p. 94).

Low technologies allow teachers to maintain control over the instructional process, and teachers do not view these technologies as mitigating their own management of the classroom. Such implements as the overhead projector, the chalkboard, and textbooks allow teachers to shape instruction in ways they deem appropriate, even if (as with textbooks) the content is prescribed. These technologies allow teachers to retain control over both management and instructional processes.

Accessibility is another key to the successful integration of technology into classroom teaching. Teachers need access to both hardware and software. The ability to preview materials is essential for planning instruction. The medium must also be adaptable to the instructional schedules of schools. Flexibility and the relatively low cost of simpler technologies contribute to their pervasiveness and accessibility for teachers. Dockterman (1988) comments on their accessibility:

> The textbook is highly portable—not just for students, but for teachers as well. They can carry it home, read it in bed, on the bus, or at the dining room table. On a simple level, the chalkboard is merely paper and pencil writ large. It is not necessary to have the board itself to prepare what will be written on it. The same is true for the overhead projector, and previously discussed equipment to produce transparencies from hard-copy pages likely increased this machine's accessibility to teachers. (p. 106)

Additionally, low technologies make no scheduling demands on teacher planning. These technologies satisfy teachers' needs instead of forcing teachers to adapt to the content and form of the medium.

 ## The Case of Computers

How do computers fare when compared with previous high and low technologies in education? Certainly, computers share many of the characteristics of the other high technologies discussed above. Their instructional use demands the acquisition of costly hardware and software. In the current age of telecommunications, school systems must also pay monthly fees for Internet access. Such cost and hardware considerations necessarily have a negative impact on accessibility. Unlike earlier high technologies, computer software and hardware rapidly become obsolete; newly developed materials often require the most recent versions of both hardware and software. In contrast, films, radio transmissions, and television broadcasts can all be viewed or heard quite effectively on older equipment. The same cannot be said for the latest computer programs or Internet technologies. The hardware and software costs associated with computers may be far more problematic than the costs of any previous educational technologies.

After examining the exorbitant costs of wiring a school for Internet access and purchasing the requisite computers and software, one might quickly decide that computers will soon suffer the same fate as other hardware-dependent technologies. Computers, however, offer several pertinent features that distinguish them from other high technologies. Computer technology changes at an incredibly rapid pace, so assumptions about today's technology may not hold for tomorrow's innovations.

Although educational software is improving in both function and content, one might argue that the available educational software has yet to meet the needs of teachers or students. In recent years several developments have created an important transformation in software. Like educational film, radio, and television, the content of educational software in the past was largely developed by an industry outside of education. As in the case of earlier technologies, software developers have devoted far greater resources to the commercial and entertainment markets. Unlike previous media, however, currently available software allows teachers and students to create their own content. With today's computer technologies, teachers can produce their own Web pages or, perhaps more important, benefit from the development of Internet resources created by other teachers. Instead of being dependent on publishers and media developers outside of education, teachers can now use telecommunication technologies to create and share their own content and resources. A genre of educational authoring software, such as Hypercard, HyperStudio, and Microworlds, also allows teachers and students to develop their own multimedia presentations. The ability to author and, with the power of the Internet, to share that work with others places the current technology in a completely different category from film, radio, and television, with their unidirectional flow of content.

Earlier high technologies touted for educational use have always put most of their resources into the commercial and entertainment markets, and the quality of their educational products has suffered accordingly. The computer and software industries have generally maintained this trend, but two specific considerations differentiate current computer technologies from the earlier high technologies. First, the content developed in other segments of the economy is now accessible to classrooms through the Internet, and teachers can integrate this content into lessons they create. For example, volumes of government documents are now available to any social studies classroom with an Internet connection. Students can access data from NASA, the current news from the *Washington Post,* or the latest stock market prices. We have entered an age where the Internet is used as a forum to announce court verdicts and to uncover political scandals. The variety and sheer volume of information available free of charge through the Internet is staggering.

Second, computer technology pervades nearly every business and professional sector of our economy. Increasingly, employees must master computer technologies to perform their jobs. The ubiquity of computers in our economy and culture puts increasing pressure on schools to produce students who are familiar with their use. As noted above, President Clinton has forecast a time when computer technologies will become an integral part of our culture, and their mastery will be essential for the functioning of our society. Students must become computer literate if they want to compete in college or at work. This type of requirement was not associated with the use of film, radio, and television in the classroom. Teachers never felt pressured to teach their students how to become functional with those technologies.

How do computers compare with the characteristics associated with the educationally successful low technologies? In terms of instructional flexibility, computers must be given a high rating. Computers can be used for statistical analysis or word processing, for graphic design or musical composition, for communicating or publishing. The rise of the Internet as a prominent feature of our culture further enhances the capability of the computer. Students can now use the same machine to both research and write papers. Classrooms and organizations can use computers to publish newsletters in paper form, or as digital Web pages for the world to read. The potential uses for computers in education seem endless; we present samples of such uses in the next chapter.

With the use of computers in the classroom, the teacher maintains control of the instructional process. Computers and the content they access, like the prose found between the covers of a textbook, are simply raw materials that teachers can use to make sense of particular classroom contexts. The teacher becomes a coach as students use the technology to investigate or create resources. The tools available with the current technologies are powerful, but the teacher must decide when, where, and how they are used. Unlike with the use of earlier high technologies, a teacher using computers must still create the objectives and plan the instruction. Computer technology increasingly promotes interactivity, in contrast to the passive approaches of film, radio, and television. Interactivity places additional control and choice in the hands of teachers and students.

Computers lend themselves to friendly scheduling in comparison with film, radio, and television. Because most of the interactions on the Internet are text based, individuals can communicate with each other over extended periods of time. Internet projects have successfully included participants in different countries without concern for individual schedules or time zones (Kent, Herbert, & McNergney, 1995). Because increasing numbers of homes have computers and access to the Internet, growing numbers of teachers and students have the option of continuing computer-based work on their own time, in their own place. Also, many public libraries provide Internet access for their patrons. Teachers can more easily preview resources at home, at the library, or in the computer lab.

Computers share some of the negative characteristics associated with the hardware and software of other high technologies, but they differ from those technologies in several important respects. As educators discover additional methods and uses for this flexible technology, computers may some day become cost-effective rather than cost-prohibitive. One test of the adaptability of computer technologies may soon come in the state of Texas. In a move to cut costs, the Texas State School Board has undertaken a study to see whether students should be furnished with laptops instead of textbooks. The chairman of the board was quoted as saying: "A year ago we replaced social studies books that still had Ronald Reagan as president, the Berlin Wall standing and the Soviet Union as one country. With laptops, you can upgrade that for $1.25" ("Texas May Drop," 1997).

If computers are able to replace textbooks, as envisioned by some members of the Texas State School Board, historians may eventually credit them as the first high technology ever to reach widespread acceptance in education. Some school systems are already taking steps toward that end. For example, 100 freshmen at Redondo Union High School in California were recently issued laptop computers that they are allowed to take home each night. This pilot program is the school's first step toward the goal of giving laptops to students across all grade levels ("Freshmen Get," 1998).

As technology increasingly encroaches upon the educational landscape, teachers are faced with the question of how to use those idle machines staring at them from the back of the room. In Chapter 4, we provide a conceptual framework for thinking about the uses of computer technology in instruction. Although there is no one right way to use technology in the classroom, the basic tenets of some proven models of instruction can be expanded to include instruction enhanced with technology. We will discuss the use of technology as applied to specific instructional models. Some real-world examples will demonstrate how these basic principles can be translated into practice.

CHAPTER FOUR

Teaching With Technology
Expanding Models of Instruction

There is nothing so practical as a good theory.
—Kurt Lewin

South East Essex College
of Arts & Technology

L ewin probably did not imagine that the glitz of technology wrapped in the hyperbole of the approaching millennium would make his words as prophetic today as they were when he uttered them in 1951. Our contemporaries who are heavily involved in computing education, however, are coming to similar conclusions. As Maddux, Johnson, and Willis (1997) note, "The use of conscious theory to guide practice would help us avoid a common, and debilitating, aspect of educational practice—fads" (p. 11). Maddux et al. felt compelled to reissue the call to reason because of what they perceive as the need to counteract "lavish claims" for computing applications. Such claims, unsubstantiated by research and theory, consist of grandiose propositions about the educational power of technology that ignore differences among learners and variations in objectives. Technology enthusiasts offer magic bullets, whereas most people don't like, don't own, and can't use technological armaments.

Simply stated, there is no one best way to use technology to educate either teachers or children. People are too different from one another, and the objectives of teaching and learning too diverse to permit the application of an all-purpose, general-effects model of teaching with technology. The so-called killer application, or killer app, that renders all learners knowledgeable, satisfied, and eager to buy more, is not out there and not likely to be. Educators need to concentrate instead on learning how to use technology in context, or matching combinations of hardware and software to the needs and abilities of learners and to the objectives of instruction.

Bruce Joyce and Marsha Weil (1972) made this claim years ago for teaching writ large. They argued that the challenge for students of teaching was not to model the master, but to master the model. With a few finely tuned strategies under his or her belt, Joyce and Weil contended, a teacher could venture forth and match these strategies to objectives and to learners. They assumed, as any reasonable person might, that a teacher could not simply "develop his or her own style" (a folkway with amazing staying power) and expect to succeed. Instead, a teacher has to demonstrate a repertoire of well-defined teaching models and be able to apply them when and where appropriate. Joyce and Weil (1996) continue to advance these eminently sensible ideas today.

Different models are meant for different purposes. Social models of teaching emphasize the relationship of the person to society or the person's direct relationships with other people. Personal models stress how the individual constructs and organizes reality, often in terms of emotions, self-concept, self-image, and personal expression. Behavioral models try to create efficient systems for sequencing learning activities and shaping behavior by manipulating reinforcement. Information-processing models help people handle stimuli from the environment, organize data, perceive problems, generate concepts and solutions to problems, and use verbal and nonverbal symbols.

What Joyce and Weil and others came to realize was that this way of thinking need not be bound by anyone's particular definition of what constitutes a model of teaching, or by any particular set of objectives, or even by any particular definition of students. Indeed, the relationships could be stated more generally: Behavior (B) is a function of the person (P) who serves as learner, the environment (E) that the teacher creates for the learner, and the tasks (T) in which the learner engages, or $B = P, E, T$ (Hunt & Sullivan, 1974; Lewin, 1935; McNergney & Carrier, 1981).

This metatheory, or theory of theories, does not prescribe exactly how the terms should be defined. Instead, it suggests only that they must be accounted for in some fashion to represent an educational system. The factors do not change simply because we begin to define any of them in part with technology. Behaviors, persons, environments, and tasks depend on each other; they constitute a "context" in which an influence on one can affect another. The implications of this way of thinking and behaving with regard to teachers and students have always been numerous, but technological innovations may enhance them dramatically.

One of the more important implications of this multivariate view of the world is that as learners vary in needs and abilities, and as the tasks they address vary, so too must educational environments differ to fit personal and task demands. No single environment can be expected to work with all people for all purposes. No one approach to teaching or teacher education—be it technologically driven or otherwise—will yield the same outcomes or behaviors in all situations. Teaching and objectives and learners and measures of success, then, must be considered together. Although teacher educators may know all of this on one level, or think they do, they all too rarely behave as though informed by these tenets.

Interestingly, however, emerging technologies may be creating the conditions that enable both teachers and teacher educators to attend to such complexities. As Figure 4.1 suggests, technology can be used to help redefine and enrich existing models of teaching by altering critical attributes of such models and by creating entirely new approaches to teaching and learning. More specifically, technology can be used to influence *tasks or objectives* that a model is meant to address, the *sequence of activities* in which teacher and learners engage, teachers' *reactions to students,* the *social system* in which teaching and learning occur, and even the *assessment* of learning. Below, we suggest how these attributes might appear in technologically rich environments.

These days, it is almost impossible to find elementary and secondary schools and institutions of higher education where the acquisition and use of technical skills are not a primary or secondary objective of instruction. These skills might range from simple keyboarding to complex interactions with people and sources of information in cyberspace. The avowed intent of many training efforts is ultimately to help learners integrate such skills into their repertoire of problem-solving abilities. The acquisition of skills and their application, then, offer new possibilities for teaching.

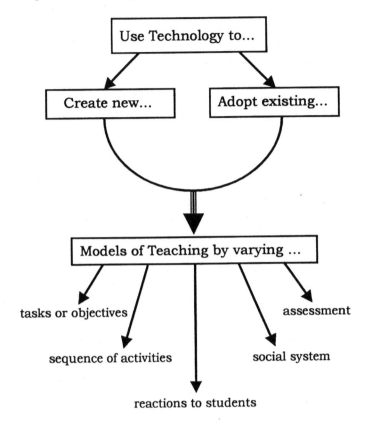

Figure 4.1. Using Technology in Context

Teaching about and with technology follows identifiable sequences of activities. For instance, teaching people how to participate in an on-line videoconference involving multiple parties requires that each party agree on the topic of the conference, prepare to air their own thinking on the issues by discussing the topic among themselves, and write several questions to ask the other parties involved. Once these preconference activities are completed, participants must identify the appropriate computer address for the on-line session. This is followed by loading and opening the videoconferencing program, adjusting camera and sound levels, and participating in turn as designated by a moderator. The success of an on-line videoconference depends heavily on teachers' and learners' capabilities to implement the appropriate sequence of activities.

Technologically speaking, there are increasing numbers of ways for teachers to react to students in on-line models of instruction. Internet- and Web-based technologies present possibilities for synchronous and asynchronous discussions, journals, video-conferences, and more. These mechanisms can be used to encourage, acknowledge, and restrict student participation. It is as if the familiar television commercial slogan for long-distance calling, "Reach out and touch someone," has finally come to teaching, but has done so in ways never before possible. What is communicated by that touch, however, is still up to the teacher.

If the social system defines the hierarchy or authority levels in a model of teaching, then a teacher has an entirely new set of technological tools to shape that hierarchy. One way to think about the social system is in terms of how technology can vary communication and privacy options to control dialogue (Bronack, 1997). At the most basic level, two or more people communicate on-line privately and selectively using e-mail and journals. A slightly more sophisticated level is represented by communication between an individual and a more intimate discussion group, where a person talks with peers who share a common interest. Yet another level of communication involves representation or advocacy—an instructor group discussion on a distance education course where the instructor represents his or her constituency to a larger group might exemplify this level. Finally, dialogue that allows little or no knowledge of the impact of one's communication—such as broadcast communications or the creation and use of a Web page—opens on-line communication among people in a fashion never before available to the average person.

Support systems are central to the implementation of any instructional model that uses technology. The hardware and software demands dictate what can and cannot be done. The capacity, flexibility, and interconnectedness of machines, programs, and people can combine to yield an array of options. The human support needed to make the hardware and software functional may be less obvious, but it is certainly no less central to teaching about and with technology. So what do these factors mean to teachers and teacher educators? If the support is not present, the options of using various models are constrained.

Educators often select and create models of teaching by concentrating on outcomes or the possible effects of instruction.

How a teacher chooses to measure his or her teaching success can be influenced by an array of technological devices. The use of electronic logs and journals, discussion groups, chat groups, and so forth yields a range of options for judging student participation and learning—options by which a model can be driven and assessed.

The point is that teachers and teacher educators, regardless of their age and technological expertise, are not ignorant of what works in teaching. They are most likely to survive and prosper in this technological age when they listen to a set of values deeply rooted in the professional knowledge of teaching, of learning, and of the content to be mastered.

From Theory to Practice

When they began their work at Teachers College, Columbia, some 30 years ago, Joyce and Weil had preservice teachers studying the theoretical underpinnings of various models and demonstrating them at the Agnes Russell Laboratory School. One could see and hear the models in a relatively undiluted state, as they existed in the controlled environment of a laboratory. This was true of other hothouse approaches to teaching and learning that were developed across the country. What people did not see, however, was the implementation of the ideal in real-life settings. That was to come later in many schools across the United States and other countries. On one hand, the transition from lab to typical schools masked the attributes of clearly defined, theoretically based models by mixing them with other naturally occurring events in classrooms. On the other hand, the mix enhanced generalizability. As the examples discussed below suggest, such are the trade-offs with dissemination of educational innovations of all kinds, including the technological variety.

Using Technology to Encourage Personal Growth

Florence McGinn's on-line journal *Electric Soup* is a collaborative Web site where young writers, singers, and poets express their personal views using a variety of media (http://www.hcrhs.hunterdon.k12.nj.us/esoup/welcome.html). Although there is much that is socially reinforcing about the site, the overriding sense one gets is of its encouraging young people to develop their personal talents and interests in a nurturing environment.

McGinn has organized the site to encourage both synchronous and asynchronous collaborations to boost personal development. Beyond the written word, photos, and audio recordings on demand, she conducts point-to-point videoconferences. These occur between writing mentors from a creative writing course at Rider College and students at Hunterdon Central Regional High School who are creating works to contribute to *Electric Soup.* In turn, students at the high school use videoconferencing to mentor middle and elementary school students contributing to the journal. In yet another variation, the HCRHS students enter peer mentoring and collaborative writing efforts with another relatively poor high school in New Jersey. Each of the schools involved has a dedicated ISDN line for the conferences. To run the sessions they use Intel Proshare software, which allows participants in the videoconferences to view each other and the work they are discussing.

Supporting Information Processing Through Technology

Marcia Linn's Knowledge Integration Environment (KIE) project at the Graduate School of Education, University of California, Berkeley (http://www.kie.berkeley.edu/KIE.html), uses emerging technologies to encourage the mastery of scientific content in middle and high school science classes. Students investigate the scientific meaning and validity of Net-based evidence, conduct scientific discussions on-line, and debate different interpretations of evidence.

Linn and her colleagues try to connect science ideas to students' lives, using a "scaffolded knowledge integration" framework. Their goal is to help students "develop an integrated scientific understanding, linking isolated scientific concepts to each other and to the world outside the science classroom." They also help students learn to use the World Wide Web, to consider Web information as evidence, and to evaluate its authorship, credibility, and relevance. Their intent is to encourage students to conduct

Some poetry written by one of McGinn's students:

Divine Intervention
his car door opened,
music falling onto the pavement
in slow-motion syrupy beats
notes dissolving on contact with
terrestrial atmosphere. if glimpsed briefly
his sequin-laden earth-tone green
leisure suit;
mirror-black sunglasses
and a grin of golden teeth
from which apostles skittered to and from,
brushing and flossing
and clamoring for words to exaggerate
into prophecy.
it's all about image, he said;
later they proclaimed his voice was thunder.

Matt Kuznicki

their own real scientific inquiry. The assumption underlying Linn's work is that students who understand science as a dynamic process, not as a static set of facts, will be more successful at learning and more likely to continue their own inquiry.

The KIE project uses on-line technologies to form partnerships between and among teachers, scientists, educational researchers, students, and parents. The KIE curriculum encourages theory comparison, critique, and the design of science projects. The KIE software implementation runs on a Mac OS computer connected to the Internet. For those who do not use Macs, there is a completely Web-based version. A Developer Center helps people adapt existing projects or create their own. A Teacher Center supports teacher use of the KIE site.

The KIE curriculum encourages students to use scientific evidence as they engage in real-life problems. KIE uses debate, critique, and design projects to complement and supplement other curricula such as laboratories.

The "All the News" Project

Project Description: All the News is a unit designed to engage students as critics and investigators as they learn scientific concepts of heat and temperature. Students are asked by the editors of a newspaper to critique Web-based scientific evidence and claims used in an article about ways to stay cool in the summertime, and to summarize their results in a letter to the editor.

Type of Project: Critique

Conceptual Learning Goals: Students should develop an improved understanding of . . . energy conversion (black materials absorb light and that light is converted to heat). Heat flow (heat flows from objects at higher temperatures to objects at lower temperatures). Thermal equilibrium (objects in the same room are the same temperature; good conductors feel colder than poor conductors because of heat flow from our bodies).

Scientific Thinking Goals: Students will learn to . . . critique evidence and claims on the basis of their scientific validity. Determine how to rephrase claims to make them scientifically valid. Appreciate the importance of thinking critically about information presented to them.

In this project, students will practice critiquing evidence using the criteria of (a) the science ideas used by the evidence, (b) methods used to create the evidence, (c) credibility of the source of the evidence, and (d) overall usefulness of the evidence.

Prerequisites: Students should be familiar with the concepts of . . . reflection, absorption, and scattering of light. Conversion of light energy into heat energy. Direction of heat flow. Thermal equilibrium.

Standard Timeframe (assuming one 50-minute period per day): 7-9 days

Target Grade Range: 7th to 10th

General Comments: Teachers should feel comfortable presenting students with problematic materials and encouraging students to use and develop inquiry skills to improve the materials. Students tend to find the project engaging, and students' understanding of energy conversion ideas significantly improves as a result of the project. Some students need extra help in differentiating between evidence and claims.

What you'll need to run this project in your classroom:

Lesson Plans: You can download a complete summary of this project, including detailed day-by-day lesson plans. You will need Adobe Acrobat Reader to view this file.

Project Files: The files for this project are included with the KIE Software, which you can get from our software download page.

A Social Example

Jeradi Hochella describes a writing project (http://pen1.pen.k12.va.us/Anthology/Div/Albemarle/Projects/Seniors) involving six elementary students who were engaged in a unique exercise in historical biography. These students used e-mail to ask questions and record conversations with senior citizens who were the subjects of the biographies the students were writing. Two of the senior citizens had access to e-mail from home, and the other four gained access through a local senior center. Students collected biographical data from the seniors and collected photographs and other memorabilia to scan digitally so that the images could be included in the biographies the students would publish on the Web.

The elementary students explored a variety of questions with their senior partners. They examined aspects of vocabulary,

---

Excerpt From the Seniors Project

When he graduated from high school in 1943, he immediately went to work at jobs that supported and produced war materials. He worked at Newark Airport where he helped in preparing fighter planes for shipment to Europe. Some of the planes he worked on were the P38 Lightning, P47 Thunderbolt, and P61 Black Widow. Mort worked 60 hours a week but still found time to see his girlfriends.

Here are some historic events that happened during his teen years:

1. Rise of Adolph Hitler.
2. Franklin D. Roosevelt began serving his first of 4 terms as president of the USA.
3. USA dropped two atomic bombs on Japan.

---

geography, and historical events. What were knickers? What was life like during the Great Depression? Where is Seneca Lake? One student learned the value of working with a living primary source; she noted, "You'd learn more than from a book because you'll learn it from their point of view." Students used traditional encyclopedias, CD-ROM reference sources, books, magazines, maps, and Web resources to help supplement the information they were receiving from their senior partners through e-mail.

As the biographies neared completion, the senior partners served as editors for accuracy as well as grammar and spelling. The seniors were pleasantly surprised to see their family pictures and images of other memorabilia throughout the text of their biographies, and the students also included images of historical events relevant to the biographies. Hochella commented on the power of "authentic" writing. She concluded: "Purposeful reasons to write provide motivation. An added measure of authenticity in this project was motivation for research." One senior had helped design the Patriot Missile. The student paired with that person made a new friend and found a new interest; the student said, "I went to the library. I went down to old magazines and found an article on the Patriot Missile."

A Behavioral Systems Example

Harry Strang's (1993, 1996, 1997) Teaching Worlds: Simulated Classroom does for teachers what they might do for students—use behavioral principles to shape desirable behavior. Strang's computer simulation allows people to teach "pupils" who appear on a computer screen. The teacher practices lesson pacing, manages student misbehavior, promotes active participation in the lesson, and provides constructive feedback to students. "These pupils will not suffer from inexperienced teachers' errors," says Strang (1993).

Written in the programming language called Visual Basic, Teaching Worlds is a menu-driven software product that runs on a DOS computer. Teaching Worlds allows teachers to practice their decision-making skills as they "teach" elementary-level children who appear on the computer screen. These children are programmed to present realistic challenges to teachers, such as

---

Teaching Worlds lists its feedback options. Below is a sample of the kind of information available.

Simulation 7: Teacher Options

During the lesson

- event status feedback is available;
- the end-lesson option is not enabled;
- think-time requests yield pupil accuracy;
- the teacher can communicate via text statements;
- lesson involvement causes pupil to stop misbehaving;
- intervention techniques maintain potency for 2 consecutive applications;
- class praise delays future misbehavior by 1 event.

Users of the software can get postlesson displays and/or printed records that allow them to review the series of teacher-pupil interactions, view the collective results of teachers' actions and pupils' responses, and evaluate the amount of time devoted to various lesson-related activities.

---

misbehaving and failing to participate. While a teacher interacts with a simulated class, the pupils respond with information relevant to the teacher's actions.

Integrating Technology Into Teacher Education

Although numerous pedagogical strategies exist for creative applications of technology in the education of the young, far less energy has been expended crafting opportunities for teachers to use technology. The National Council for the Accreditation of Teacher Education (NCATE) has drawn attention to some of the more notable examples (see Case Illustrations of Technology in Teacher Education at the NCATE site http://www.ncate.org/projects/tech/).

In teacher education as well as in the education of children, there is considerable interest in the idea of making technology "transparent," or integrating it into educational activities. The intent is to promote the acquisition of technology skills as a secondary rather than a primary instructional objective. One way to do this is to encourage the use of technology in pursuit of other educational goals. In using technology to address these goals, then, a person naturally or transparently acquires new or improved technology skills. We have used this backdoor approach to encouraging the development of technology skills while advancing a primary agenda of the development of case analysis skills or educational problem-solving abilities in a program called CaseNET.

CaseNET is a set of case-based, Internet-based courses for teachers created and managed by faculty and graduate students at the University of Virginia (http://casenet.edschool.virginia.edu). The courses focus on three areas: interdisciplinary teaching and learning, standards of learning and assessment, and using technology to solve problems in schools. Working from multimedia scenarios that capture real classroom life, preservice and inservice teachers learn to apply a case study method that includes five steps that form the foundation for making judgments in teaching and learning situations: identifying key issues, recognizing multiple perspectives, examining available knowledge, forecasting possible actions, and predicting their effects.

CaseNET brings together an ever-growing community of school systems, colleges, and universities from across the United States and around the world.

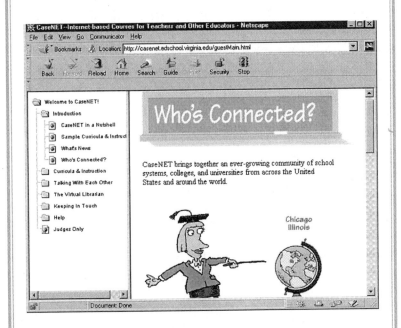

Course content is delivered to teachers, aides, and school administrators in a case-based format via the Internet (World Wide Web, videoconference, discussion groups, and electronic mail), videotape, and print materials. Faculty build on their previous work with case-method teaching and learning, and on similar approaches in business, law, and medicine, to bring knowledge to bear on problems in schools. CaseNET is not distance education in the typical sense; that is, instructors meet with students at respective sites and hold classes on a regular basis. The assumption is that the ultimate success of a CaseNET offering still depends primarily on the teacher educator who is live, on site.

CaseNET encourages participants to (a) use the Internet and Web technologies to solve educational problems or "cases" as they emerge in elementary, middle, and high schools; (b) cooperate within teams and compare analyses across teams in search of solutions to cases; (c) link with people from other sites via Internet videoconference and discussion groups to concentrate on case issues; (d) write their own cases for use in school-embedded staff development and for use with students in their classrooms; and (e) practice solving problems in ways that help to prepare them to continue professional development on the job.

Conclusion

We have said only that technologies might help enhance the matching of educational environments to the characteristics of learners, be they young people or teachers. But we have not said much about the characteristics of the people themselves. Certainly it seems reasonable to expect that people's values, prior knowledge, preferred sensory modalities, attitudes toward change, anxiety, motivation, and maybe even age will influence their susceptibility to educational environments that are technologically driven. It is unlikely that all people will react in the same way to the same educational approach. Teacher educators might profitably spend some time unraveling the complexities of which approach might benefit which persons and in what ways.

We have also suggested that using technologies in various combinations can enrich existing educational models and lead to the creation of some entirely new approaches to teaching and learning. When we think about how technology can allow teachers and teacher educators to connect people and ideas in new ways, the revelation of previously unimagined models of educational practice seems likely. When children grow up around technologies, make those technologies part of their lives, and cooperate with one another in their use, new models are bound to emerge. As they do, we might see the innovations first by looking back over our shoulders. Virtually speaking, the kid coming up fast behind us in the outside lane just might be the one who makes us rethink the whole enterprise.

CHAPTER FIVE

Envisioning Future Uses of Educational Technology
Currency in a Rapidly Changing World

A scholar asked Alfred North Whitehead which he believed to be more important, ideas or things. "Why, I should imagine ideas about things," Whitehead replied.

The magic lantern—a forerunner of the modern slide projector—was introduced into the classroom in the nineteenth century with the promise of bringing the "world" to students through the projection of spectacular images onto the classroom wall. Like so many other technologies, the bright promise of the magic lantern dimmed with time, and the apparatus eventually disappeared from the classroom. Time and again, technologies either have failed to prove their value to classroom teachers or have been replaced by newer technologies. In schools across the country, filmstrip projectors, Betamax videocassette players, reel-to-reel tape recorders, videodisk players, and Commodore computers are collecting dust in dark storage areas. Modern computer technologists also claim they will bring the "world" into our children's classrooms, but computer technologies change seemingly overnight. Virtual museums of obsolete computer technologies can already be toured on the World Wide Web, and today's hottest technologies seem to cool all too rapidly. Teacher educators must train tomorrow's teachers in a rapidly changing world with an increasingly uncertain future. What role might we expect technology to play in future classrooms? Will technology transform how we view teaching, or are new technologies destined to serve simply as supplementary resources, as in the case of movies or videotapes? In this chapter we examine what the future may bring to the world of teacher education. Good ideas, not necessarily new technological developments, guide the way.

Current computer technologies are remarkable in their versatility. Computer programs can be used for doing tax returns or writing poetry. The same computer can be used to videoconference with someone across the world or to find a book in the local library. The possibilities seem endless. To some extent, teacher educators must peer into the future and determine what skills and knowledge their students will need to work effectively in their classrooms. Because computer technologies change so rapidly, teaching skills tied to specific applications will have only limited long-term value. Students who see technology modeled in the classes they attend and who have opportunities to apply technology in their own teaching will be more likely to learn and apply the new technologies they encounter. As we noted in Chapter 4, the $B = P, E, T$ formula is one way to think about the complexity of forces that contribute to learning. The tasks (T) that are possible with new technologies 5 years from now will be very different from the tasks that are possible today. Moreover, the school environments (E) in which teachers will find themselves in the future might be entirely different from what teachers experience today. Instead of learning specific technological skills or accomplishing discrete tasks, tomorrow's teachers might usefully spend time dealing academically and practically with the interplay of these variables. An understanding of the relationships, grounded in hands-on experience, could help teachers adapt their work to the specific contexts they will find in classrooms.

One of the technologies that has shown the most resilience to change is the printed word. Since the printing of the Gutenberg Bible in 1455 (a reproduction of which is now available on CD-ROM, and selected pages of which are viewable on the World Wide Web), printed texts have been the primary medium for learning and the exchange of ideas. The printed word, however, could be largely replaced by the digitized word. The impetus for this change, as with many changes in education, is economic. In Chapter 3, we gave the example of a Texas school system that is considering the use of laptops to combat the high cost of textbooks. To illustrate the point further, Noam (1998) describes the volume of work that scholarly journals must manage:

> To get a sense of the quantitative trend: Chemical Abstracts took 30 years (1907-1937) to reach its first one million abstracts. The second million took 18 years. The most recent million took only 1.75 years. Thus, more articles on chemistry have been published in the past 2 years than in humankind's entire history before 1900. . . . Meanwhile, the prices for journals keep getting higher, as specialization reduces circulation to ever-narrower slivers of specialists, and as commercial publishers consolidate profitably. (p. 4)

As human knowledge continues a pattern of increasing specialization, technology may be the only recourse for managing the rapid growth of information. Technology could transform the most basic tools used by teachers, and this transformation might also create radically new types of learning environments.

Developers at the Massachusetts Institute of Technology, for example, are experimenting with technologies for creating an electronic textbook. The pages of the book will contain e-ink, which is basically a grid of microscopic spheres that are half white and half black. These spheres can flip to either color as determined by an electronic current running through the page in a network of extremely fine wires. A microcomputer in the spine of the book will allow readers to select, simply by pushing buttons, what text they want to appear on the pages of e-ink. These electronic books will retain the feel and readability of paper pages, yet the developers believe that the technology will eventually allow entire libraries of texts to be stored in a single volume. A prototype with just a few pages might be ready in only 2 to 3 years (Lehmann-Haupt, 1998). Having such enormous resources at students' fingertips in the classroom would necessarily change the types of learning activities that take place.

The classroom of tomorrow will be different in terms of the types of information available to students. Such a classroom is described by school superintendent Ray Farley as follows:

> As you enter the Classroom of the Future, you will see and feel an energy and excitement that parallels the world around us. Students have instantaneous access to limitless resources throughout the world. There will be 6 to 12 computers in the room. Aligned desks and chairs have been replaced by conference tables and work areas equipped with laptops and a telephone; books have been replaced by CD-ROMs and laser disks. The students will be directing their own learning as the teacher facilitates. Many of the activities in which the students are engaged will look very different than those that may have taken place in the classroom we attended in the past. (Farley, in Farley, Gray, & Pare, 1996, p. 20)

He goes on:

> The Classroom of the Future is not a room. Learning takes place 24 hours a day; students direct their own learning when and where they need to learn. Resources include parents, community members, and online experts who mentor the learners when the traditional school day ends. There is no longer a single evaluator of student performance in a classroom—the world becomes the classroom. (p. 21)

Emerging technologies open many possibilities for greater individualization and student-directed learning. As technologies bring the "world" into the classroom, the distinction between the classroom and the "world" begins to blur. The notion of a conventional classroom becomes antiquated and perhaps even obsolete. Are such classrooms merely futuristic musings?

Horizon Instructional Systems is the largest nonconversion charter school in California and has more than 1,600 students. Yet the school has no permanent classrooms. The basic concept, as outlined in the school's 1997 charter, is that learning is completely individualized:

Parents and their children work with their education specialist to determine their educational goals and objectives, to create their individualized curriculum, and to determine their individual methods of teaching and learning. The parent will have the right to determine the degree to which the education specialist is involved. This involvement may vary from an advisory and assessment capacity to one of almost complete administration of the student learning process. Each parent facilitator is required to sign a contract between the parent and the charter school stipulating the distribution between the parent facilitator and the education specialist. (Horizon Instructional Systems, 1997)

Each Horizon education specialist has California teaching credentials. The specialist is budgeted money for each student, and the allotment must be spent entirely on the student's instructional program. Each education specialist has a maximum of 37 students, all of whom live in close geographic proximity. Students can work closely with parents in a "home schooling" environment, or they may work primarily with their education specialist. If a family is unhappy with a particular specialist, another is assigned. Each student has free Internet access from home. Computer technology links the students with the school and to learning resources. Each education specialist draws materials from the school, in a procedure similar to library loans, for each student, and all orders and materials are tracked with laptops given to each specialist. Curriculum catalogs, chat areas, bulletin boards, and school newsletters are all available through the school's Web site. If students are interested in small-group instruction on a particular topic, the school's bulletin board coordinates interested parties and resources. Chat room classes and "whiteboard" technologies are often used for math problem solving. Members of the school community are listed by expertise, to serve as resources for students. The school offers 230 classes to 1,700 students from six different counties. The school budget for each student is approximately $3,300.

The highly individualized vision of education represented by Horizon Instructional Systems might be an educational harbinger. Does such a vision mean the end of public education? "Yes," says

Lewis Perelman; "Absolutely not," says Ray Farley, superintendent of the Hunterton Central Regional School district. Perelman's vision of "microvouchers" offers the means for replacing public schooling as we know it. Individuals will pay for learning on an "as needed" basis through their computerized learning environments. Farley has applauded Horizon's innovative use of technology for individualized learning, but he cautions pundits like Perelman and charter school advocates not to underestimate the competitive spirit of public schools. Farley believes all education in the future, whether public or otherwise, will have to be flexible, portable, and low cost to compete. Public schools are beginning to "wake up" to this reality. Some public schools now outpace higher education in their use of technology.[1]

If technology will change the schools of tomorrow, how will institutions of higher education fare? Perelman predicts they will become obsolete. When asked what he would do if he were in the position of a college president, he replied:

> I would get rid of all the old buildings and bricks and mortar and grounds and go virtual, but not go virtual just to become a more efficient diploma mill, which I think is a loser, but to really focus on what I think the market wants, which is know-how. I would create a know-how market. And probably I would drop the name university or college—because the new business, whatever it is, the new institution is not an educational institution. And the customer knows that. To the extent that they want this new thing called "kanbrain," called "hyperlearning"—call it whatever you want—they know it's not "school." If they want school, they want to be in the top five percent, they want a diploma, they want to be an alumnus, they want to have a football team—and, you know, if they want all that stuff, they don't want it on a TV set. (quoted in Educom Review Staff, 1997, pp. 4-5)[2]

Perelman's vision and the instructional philosophy behind Horizon Instructional Systems emphasizes highly individualized learning at the expense of a more social learning environment. Perelman responds to this criticism:

> When I talk about hyperlearning and distance-learning and all this new-fangled stuff, somebody inevitably says, yes,

> that's very nice but it's never going to be as good as the gifted teacher in a classroom or the personal experience of going to Oxford or Harvard or whatever. They keep talking about experience, they love that word experience. Well look at this situation in 1952 again. I put the pictures of the SS United States up on the wall, the picture of the Comet jet plane, and ask the question: Which is better? Well, it depends to what purpose. If you need to be in Paris tomorrow morning to sign a contract, close a deal, there is no question; the plane is not just the better option, it is really the only option. If you want to enjoy the "experience" of luxury and entertainment, the steamship, with its swimming pools, restaurants, night clubs, movie theaters, sunshine, fresh air and all that, is incomparably better. (p. 2)

Perelman reduces the face-to-face social interactions of contemporary schooling to an expensive luxury. Technology may someday facilitate cheaper, more individualized instruction, but whether such a vision of education is "better" depends on the purpose of that education. Certainly, technology need not replace social interaction in the classroom. Simply because virtual learning environments can be created does not mean the use of technology and classroom-based learning are mutually exclusive. Norman (1992) summarizes the importance of the social context:

> Experience with technology teaches us that once a technology makes something possible, it gets applied, whether good or bad. It makes sense to be able to show a sixth grade play to interested relatives. . . . It makes no sense to destroy the experience through the act of recording it. It makes sense to have control over the viewing of records. It makes no sense to sacrifice human social relations in the process. Which will it be? I put my faith in people. Human social interaction is too important, too fundamental, to fall to obstructionist artifacts and event fanatics. (p. 14)

Radio, television, and film never seriously threatened to usurp the teacher's position as guiding light in the classroom. The instructional success of those technologies depended heavily on the types of classroom interactions that took place, under the auspices of the teacher, in reaction to the content presented by the media.

Proponents of the earlier technologies soon realized that the successful use of the technologies depended directly on teachers' skills in integrating the technologies with classroom activities. Too often this realization turned to blame as teachers were held responsible for any and all shortcomings of the technologies and their implementation in the schools. Teaching and learning are based on human interactions. Removing the personal aspect of education, or the "experience," as Perelman describes it, may have consequences that are difficult to predict. Despite Perelman's vehement condemnation of the existing educational system, the "know-how" he values so highly in the business world translates to working, learning, and producing in a social work environment. What is done, learned, and produced depends heavily on the environment, the tasks performed, and the people involved—not unlike the classroom. Removing the experience of performing tasks in a social context may have costs that Perelman and others mistakenly undervalue. Even some in the computer industry have voiced such concerns:

> Hewlett-Packard chairman Lewis E. Platt has some worries about the way the Internet may be developing: "Technology has made our society a little less personal, and this trend will only increase as more and more interactions move into the electronic world" and, like television, begin to "dull our senses, reduce our attention spans, convert intellectual conversations into sound bites." The Internet "could change the way that we educate and learn. It could eliminate the boundaries of time and space, and it could bring our world together. But as the Internet becomes more pervasive, as it becomes more commercial, it runs the risk of making our world worse, instead of better." (Holsendolph, 1998)

The best way to safeguard against the "dulling of our senses" is to use the technology effectively. Teachers, and teacher educators, are the individuals who are most capable of sorting out educational forces at work in schools. No single model, no one software application, no solitary course can help students fully appreciate these relationships. By working within an environment that models the effective use of technology, by learning technical and instructional skills in context, and by having opportunities to apply those skills in their own teaching, students have a chance to adapt and transfer their learning to other situations. The instructional use of technology is most likely to succeed if teachers can adapt and help others do the same (Hess & McNergney, 1998).

Perelman's vision of an apocalyptic end to education as we know it parallels some of the claims made by Edison for the potential of previous technologies to revolutionize classroom teaching. Those technologies never experienced large or lasting effects on classroom instruction. In the main, they failed because they lacked the capacity to provide a range of options that could be fitted to classroom situations. Contemporary computer technologies have the flexibility to be used in a variety of ways for a variety of purposes. The teacher, however, still bears responsibility for their use. Just as models of teaching are malleable, so too can new technologies shape and be shaped by others. The promise of success, however, resides in the decisions and actions of the teacher in employing the technologies within an instructional framework.

Teachers and teacher educators must look beyond current rhetoric and hyperbole to the potential of technology as part of a teacher's repertoire. At the same time, they might prudently resist the prognostications of self-proclaimed prophets who discount the importance and power of these technologies. The current situation is strikingly similar to the conditions that surrounded the invention of the first computer in the 19th century. Coinventor Ada Byron observed:

> It is desirable to guard against the possibility of exaggerated ideas that might arise as to the powers of the Analytical Engine. In considering any new subject, there is frequently a tendency, first, to overrate what we find to be already interesting or remarkable; and, secondly, by a sort of natural reaction, to undervalue the true state of the case, when we do discover that our notions have surpassed those that were really tenable. The Analytical Engine has no pretensions whatever to originate any thing. It can do whatever we know how to order it to perform. It can follow analysis; but it has no power of anticipating any analytical relations or truths. Its province is to assist us in making available what we are already acquainted with. (quoted in Toole, 1992, p. 722)

Perhaps in the final analysis, computers in education will do exactly that: make available in new ways the content and instructional models we are already acquainted with.

Some educators believe that the media used for instruction exert primarily an economic dimension—in terms of saving time or cost—over instruction. The learning outcomes are determined by the instructional framework, not the media. Clark (1994) argues that instructional outcomes are not tied to any one medium of instruction. He writes that instructional media are "mere vehicles that deliver instruction but do not influence student achievement any more than the truck that delivers our groceries causes changes in our nutrition" (p. 23). To Clark, then, student achievement depends on instructional method and other factors. He would contend that the results from technology use should be tied solely to the instructional method employed with the technology, not to any particular attribute associated with the technology. Because he believes that the type of medium is largely irrelevant to instructional outcomes, Clark suggests that cost and access should be the primary factors considered in deciding which medium to use.

If we accept Clark's premise, decisions can be based on the cost, effectiveness, and other practical considerations of individual instructional packages. We need not worry about so-called instructional effects of technology. Educators must be able to make informed decisions in choosing the appropriate media for given instructional tasks.

The CaseNET project, described in Chapter 4, has succeeded primarily because its instructional framework is built upon a case-based methodology proven effective in a variety of environments. The CaseNET technology is a combination of cost-effective media that bring together students from distant institutions to reflect on a common body of content. The media allow cases to be developed in a nonlinear format, incorporating video and audio to supplement information embedded in text. Perhaps more than any other aspect of the project, the success of CaseNET depends on the expertise of the instructors at each of the remote sites. Although the technology delivers content and provides a forum for the exchange of ideas, the instructors create the learning environments that enable students to work together productively. Removing this human element from the CaseNET equation would reduce the course to an inert body of information archived on the Web.

Perelman's vision of student-directed learning on demand mistakenly devalues the human experience in education. Believing students can shape their own learning productively simply because they have access to a digital network is equivalent to turning students loose in a library and expecting them to benefit spontaneously from the vast resources contained on the shelves. Real teachers know that content represents only an opportunity for learning; learning occurs when students engage the content. Models provide proven frameworks for such engagement, and current technologies are vehicles for applying these frameworks to new contexts found in modern classrooms. As with every other technology that has emerged on the educational landscape, ultimately the teacher will establish the value of the computer in learning.

 Notes

1. These remarks are based upon Farley's participation in a presentation at a regional conference on public school choice sponsored by the New Jersey Institute for School Innovation, held at Princeton University on March 14, 1998.

2. This material and the following quote are reprinted by permission of *Educom Review*.

 # References

Apple Computer, Inc. (1995). *Changing the conversation about teaching, learning, and technology: A report on 10 Years of ACOT research.* Cupertino, CA: Author.

Applebome, P. (1997, February 7). Clinton calls for new deal in education. *New York Times* [On-line]. Available: http://www.nytimes.com

Beichner, R. J. (1993). Technology competencies for new teachers: Issues and suggestions. *Journal of Computing in Teacher Education, 9*(3), 17-20.

Bronack, S. C. (1997, December). *Levels of discourse within a Web-based collaborative learning environment.* Paper presented at the Computer Support for Collaborative Learning conference, Toronto.

Byrum, D. C., & Cashman, C. (1993). Preservice teacher training in educational computing: Problems, perceptions, and preparation. *Journal of Technology and Teacher Education, 1,* 259-274.

Clark, R. E. (1994). Media will never influence learning. *Educational Technology Research and Development, 42*(2), 21-29.

Clinton, W. J. (1996, August). [Address to the Democratic National Convention]. Available: http://www.pub.whitehouse.gov/uri-res/I2R?urn:pdi://oma.eop.gov.us/1996=/9/4/13.text.1

Clinton, W. J. (1997, February 5). The State of the Union address [Transcript]. *New York Times.*

Cooper, J. M., & Bull, G. L. (1997). Technology and teacher education: Past practice and recommended directions. *Action in Teacher Education, 9*(2), 97-106.

Cuban, L. (1986). *Teacher and machines: The classroom use of technology since 1920.* New York: Teachers College Press.

Darrow, B. (1932). *Radio: The assistant teacher.* Columbus, OH: R. G. Adams.

Dockterman, D. A. (1988). *Tools for teachers: An historical analysis of classroom technology.* Unpublished doctoral dissertation, Harvard University.

Dwyer, D. C., Ringstaff, C., & Sandholtz, J. H. (1990). *Teacher beliefs and practices: Part I. Patterns of change* [Apple Classrooms of Tomorrow Research Report No. 8] [On-line]. Available: http://www.research.apple.com/technology/proj/acot/full/acotRpt08full.html

Educom Review Staff. (1997). Barnstorming with Lewis Perelman. *Educom Review* [On-line], *32*(2). Available: http://www.educom.edu/ web/pubs/review/reviewArticles/32218.html

Farley, R. P., Gray, J., & Pare, R. (1996, July/August). The classroom of the future. *School Leader,* pp. 20-21.

Freshmen get take-home laptops. (1998, March 14). *Los Angeles Times* [On-line], p. B2. Available: http:/www.latimes.com

Gough, P. B. (1998, May). Short memories. *Phi Delta Kappan,* p. 642.

Hess, F. M., & McNergney, R. F. (1998, March). Technology trade-offs. *Electronic School,* pp. A30-A33.

Holsendolph, E. (1998, March 22). Commercialism threat to Web, H-P chief says. *Atlanta Journal-Constitution.*

Horizon Instructional Systems. (1997). Horizon School charter. Available: http://www.nccn.net/hnycmbpd/Horizon/estabdoc/charter.html

Hunt, D. E., & Sullivan, E. V. (1974). *Between psychology and education.* Hinsdale, IL: Dryden.

Joyce, B., & Weil, M. (1972). *Models of teaching.* Englewood Cliffs, NJ: Prentice Hall.

Joyce, B., & Weil, M. (1996). *Models of teaching* (2nd ed.). Boston: Allyn & Bacon.

Kent, T. W., Herbert, J. M., & McNergney, R. F. (1995). Telecommunications in teacher education: Reflections on the first virtual team case competition. *Journal of Information Technology for Teacher Education, 4*(2), 137-148.

Lehmann-Haupt, C. (1998, April 8). Creating "the last book" to hold all the others. *New York Times* [On-line]. Available: http://www.nytimes.com

Lewin, K. (1935). *A dynamic theory of personality.* New York: McGraw-Hill.

Maddux, C. D., Johnson, D. L., & Willis, J. W. (1997). *Educational computing: Learning with tomorrow's technologies* (2nd ed.). Boston: Allyn & Bacon.

McNergney, R. F., & Carrier, C. A. (1981). *Teacher development.* New York: Macmillan.

Milken Family Foundation. (1997). *Preparing our young people for a changing world: A Milken exchange on education technology* [Press release]. Santa Monica, CA: Author.

National Council for Accreditation of Teacher Education. (1997). *Technology and the new professional teacher: Preparing for the 21st century classroom.* Washington, DC: Author.

Noam, E. M. (1998). Will books become the dumb medium? *Educom Review, 32*(2), 1-7.

Norman, D. A. (1992). *Turn signals are the facial expressions of automobiles.* Reading, MA: Addison-Wesley.

Office of Technology Assessment. (1995). *Teachers and technology: Making the connection.* Washington, DC: Government Printing Office.

Perelman, L. J. (1993). *School's out: A radical new formula for the revitalization of America's educational system.* New York: Avon.

Persichitte, K. A. (1998). *Examples of best practice in the use and integration of educational technologies for K-12 teacher preparation.* Presentation at the Ninth International Meeting of the Society for Information Technology and Teacher Education, Washington, DC.

Persichitte, K. A., Tharp, D. D., & Caffarella, E. P. (1997). *The use of technology by schools, colleges, and departments of education.* Washington, DC: American Association of Colleges for Teacher Education.

President's Committee of Advisors on Science and Technology. (1997, March). *Report to the president on the use of technology to strengthen K-12 education in the United States.* Washington, DC: Government Printing Office.

Saettler, P. (1990). *The evolution of American educational technology.* Englewood, CO: Libraries Unlimited.

Strang, H. R. (1993). *Teaching worlds: Simulated classroom challenges.* Boston: Allyn & Bacon.

Strang, H. R. (1996). The TD simulation: An interactive vehicle for mapping teaching decisions. *Journal of Technology and Teacher Education, 4,* 133-143.

Strang, H. R. (1997). The use of Curry teaching simulations in professional training. *Computers in the Schools, 13,* 135-145.

Technology counts [Press release]. (1997a, November 10). Washington, DC: Education Week.

Technology counts [Special issue]. (1997b, November 10). *Education
Week, 17*(11). Available: http://www.edweek.org/sreports/tc/

Texas may drop all textbooks, for laptops. (1997, November 19). *New
York Times* [On-line]. Available: http://www.nytimes.com

Thomas, L., Larson, A., Clift, R. T., & Levin, J. (1996). Integrating technology in teacher education programs: Lessons from the Teaching
Teleapprenticeships Project. *Action in Teacher Education, 17*(4),
1-8.

Toole, B. A. (1992). *Ada, the enchantress of numbers.* Mill Valley, CA:
Strawberry. Available: http://www.cs.yale.edu/homes/tap/Files/
ada-lovelace-notes.html

Trotter, A. (1997, November 10). Taking technology's measure. *Education Week, 17*(11). Available: http://www.edweek.org/sreports/tc/

Trotter, A., & Zehr, M. A. (1998, March 11). More schools, classrooms
gaining access to Internet. *Education Week* [On-line]. Available:
http://www.edweek.org

Tyack, D., & Cuban, L. (1995). *Tinkering toward utopia: A century of
public school reform.* Cambridge, MA: Harvard University Press.

Viadero, D. (1997a, November 10). Putting it all together. *Education
Week, 17*(11), 16. Available: http://www.edweek.org/sreports/tc/

Viadero, D. (1997b, November 10). A tool for learning. *Education
Week, 17*(11), 12-13, 15, 17-18. Available: http://www.edweek.org/
sreports/tc/

Wagschal, P. H. (1986). Computers in the schools: Lessons from television. *Curriculum Review, 25*(3), 32-34.

Zehr, M. A. (1997). Teaching the teachers. *Education Week, 17*(11), 24-
29. Available: http://www.edweek.org/sreports/tc/

Index

CORWIN
PRESS